OYSTER
GASTRONOMY

In memory of a dear friend, photographer,
and ostreaphile extraordinaire,
Walter Pfeiffer.

First published in Ireland 2017
by Artisan House Ltd., Letterfrack, Connemara,
County Galway, Ireland.
w w w . a r t i s a n h o u s e . i e

Co-authors	**Máirín Uí Chomáin**
	Michael O'Meara
Creative	**Vincent Murphy**
Editorial	**Mary Ruddy**
Photography	**Walter Pfeiffer**
	Michael O'Meara
Foreword	**Richard Donnelly**
Beverage notes	**Betty Murphy**
Copy-editor	**Stan Carey**
Proofreader and indexer	**Kate Murphy**
Printing	**Imago**

Design & editing © Artisan House Connemara 2017
Recipes & text © Máirín Uí Chomáin 2017
Recipes, text & photography © Michael O'Meara 2017
Photography © Estate of Walter Pfeiffer 2017
Foreword © Richard Donnelly 2017
Beverage notes © Betty Murphy 2017

Oysters by Seamus Heaney from Field Work 1979
by kind permission of **Faber & Faber Ltd**

ISBN **978 0 9926908 7 8**

A CIP catalogue record for this book is available
from the British Library.

Papers used in the production of *Oyster Gastronomy*
are made from wood grown in sustainable forests

Native oyster beds in Galway Bay

OYSTER
GASTRONOMY

Máirín Uí Chomáin & Michael O'Meara

Photography by
Walter Pfeiffer &
Michael O'Meara

ARTISAN HOUSE
PUBLISHING

Books of *taste* Created with *passion* In the heart of *Connemara*

Oysters

Our shells clacked on the plates.
My tongue was a filling estuary,
My palate hung with starlight:
As I tasted the salty Pleiades
Orion dipped his foot into the water.

Alive and violated,
They lay on their beds of ice:
Bivalves: the split bulb
And philandering sigh of ocean.
Millions of them ripped and shucked and scattered.

We had driven to that coast
Through flowers and limestone
And there we were, toasting friendship,
Laying down a perfect memory
In the cool of thatch and crockery.

Over the Alps, packed deep in hay and snow,
The Romans hauled their oysters south to Rome:
I saw damp panniers disgorge
The frond-lipped, brine-stung
Glut of privilege

And was angry that my trust could not repose
In the clear light, like poetry or freedom
Leaning in from the sea. I ate the day
Deliberately, that its tang
Might quicken me all into verb, pure verb.

Seamus Heaney (1939–2013)

Contents

Foreword Richard Donnelly

Was there ever a food that created such a mixed reaction as the humble oyster, from 'Oh, I could never eat that!' to the ostreaphile's childlike enthusiasm and drooling anticipation upon opening one of these treasures? Fortunately for ostreaphiles, the experience never ceases to bring wonder and a vast range of taste experiences. Every newly opened oyster is a voyage of discovery for the senses, and this is just one reason for the constant journey to taste oysters from different locations.

Two types of oyster are cultivated in Ireland: the native European oyster, or flat oyster (*Ostrea edulis*), and the Irish rock oyster, or cupped or Pacific oyster (*Crassostrea gigas*). The Irish rock oyster was introduced to Ireland in the late 1970s and now predominates, accounting for over 95% of all production in the country. The two species have very different tastes, and oysters from different bays have distinctive flavours. Similar to wine, location provides its own unique taste. This is what oyster lovers call the 'meroir'. Globally, *Crassostrea gigas* is the number one species of

farmed oyster, with most production in China. Other species farmed around the world include the American oyster (*Crassostrea virginica*), Sydney rock oyster (*Saccostrea glomerata*) and Southern mud oyster (*Ostrea angasi*).

The whole art of oyster tasting is to identify the subtle flavours that the growing environment produces in the flesh of the oyster. Consumption of oysters raw is often favoured as the best method, because it helps to reveal these flavours. Like a wine connoisseur, the ostreaphile will describe taste in terms of brine, tannic, cucumber and a myriad of other aspects of these complex flavours. And like wine tasting, it's all about what you enjoy – leave the hyperbole to those who enjoy such endeavours of the palate.

Whichever way you enjoy your oysters, one thing is certain: they are an extremely healthy seafood. Oysters are rich in protein, low in fat, and contain high levels of the essential minerals iodine, iron, selenium, copper and zinc. A portion of six oysters provides you with the daily recommended levels of these trace minerals.

The health benefits did not go unnoticed by earlier generations. There is extensive evidence, in shell mittens from around the coast of Ireland, of oyster consumption dating back over 5,000 years. This would have been the native European oyster, and we get snippets of information about it in the following centuries – most notably around the 1500s, when we begin to see increased management of these wild fisheries. In 1595 the city corporation of Dublin asked for gravel and stones to be laid to provide a suitable substrate for juvenile oysters to settle on in Poolbeg. 1614 saw the first recorded importation of oysters, with stocks taken from Milford Haven to Bannow Bay.

This practice of supplementing stocks continued, and by the mid-nineteenth century there was significant movement of stocks around the globe. We get an insight into this in 1838 when the famous oyster beds of Clontarf were stocked with oysters from America and France. These American oysters are the same species, *Crassostrea virginica*, farmed to this day in much of North America.

The constant movement of stocks to fattening beds continued throughout the 1800s. During this time we see an increasing commercial aspect to oyster fisheries and movement towards what could be called extensive farming. This led to greater exploitation, and stocks in all major fisheries in Ireland, Britain and France began to suffer. In Ireland, licences were issued all around the coast in an effort to control, monitor and preserve the remaining stocks. The extent of the industry can be seen from one observer who reports over 50 boats and 200 men engaged in the Clew Bay Fishery in 1835.

But the big change to the Irish industry came in the following decade with the arrival of railways. In the past, oysters from around Ireland were transported to the lucrative markets of London and other cities in England mainly by steamer and sailing ships. Now oysters could be transported rapidly from all corners of Ireland directly to ferry ports in Dublin and quickly onward to their destinations in Britain. Oysters were also being sent to supplement the depleted fisheries in England and France. Large quantities of half-grown oysters were taken particularly from the east coast of Ireland for restocking abroad. Licensed owners were acutely aware of the impending depletion of their fisheries, and numerous attempts were made to alleviate the predicament. This included importing American, French, Dutch and Portuguese oysters. Attempts were also made to spawn oysters artificially, most notably in 1903 at the Ardfry Experimental Oyster Cultivation Station in Galway. But it was in vain – all the native and Irish stocks were in critical condition at the start of the twentieth century. This situation prevailed until the 1950s despite sporadic attempts to restore some sites.

Bord Iascaigh Mhara (BIM), Ireland's sea fisheries board, was established in July 1952. At this time only the Tralee Bay, Galway Bay and Clew Bay oyster fisheries were of any significance – and they were a shadow of what they had been. It was not until 1967 that a great leader of the Irish oyster industry arrived from Wales to work for BIM. Dr Eric Edwards would become instrumental in driving the modern shellfish industry in Ireland, and was a pioneer in rescuing the Galway Bay stocks from probable extinction.

France, like Ireland, had its native oyster industry decimated and had investigated ways to preserve this vital industry and tradition. After some success with the Portuguese oyster (*Crassostrea angulata*) in the 1950s and '60s, the French industry switched totally to the species we are familiar with today, known by a range of local names such as Pacific or Japanese oyster (*Crassostrea gigas*). It was grown very successfully in France, and also in Canada, so in the early 1970s Ireland looked at this species to rejuvenate its moribund oyster industry.

Today this oyster is the main species grown in both Ireland and France, Ireland having adopted many of the techniques of the French industry. In fact, in the 1980s and '90s, French operators were the key to expansion of the industry, which now flourishes all around the coast of Ireland. Production is approaching 10,000 tonnes annually, or about 90 million oysters a year: very impressive when compared with the famous Arklow Banks fishery of 1863, which harvested about 30 million oysters annually.
The key difference is that the current oyster cultivation business is fully sustainable. Irish rock oysters cannot propagate successfully in Irish

waters, as the sea temperatures are too low. But they do go through the spawning phase and can become 'milky' during the summer months. In order to maintain the stocks, Irish rock oysters are first grown in specialised hatcheries with suppliers in Ireland, UK and France. Hatcheries in France and in the USA have led the way in genetic breeding. They have successfully crossed a tetraploid oyster (one with four sets of chromosomes) with a diploid (two sets) to produce an oyster commonly referred to in the industry as a triploid (three sets). This oyster is ideal for growing, as it does not enter the spawning phase and is in effect sterile. Most oysters grown in Ireland are triploid; they produce excellent meats and can be eaten all year round.

The Irish industry was also influenced by French growing techniques, whereby oysters are placed in specially designed bags on top of trestles (metal frames). This keeps the oysters off the sea bed and away from predators such as starfish and crabs. The connection with France continues, as it is the main export market for Irish oysters. Many of them are bathed briefly in French waters, and voila: they become French oysters. Recently, Ireland has also gained a reputation for top-quality oysters in Asian markets. Every day, oysters are flown directly to locations such as Singapore, Shanghai and Hong Kong and served at top prices to discerning customers.

Although oysters are grown all around the Irish coast, two bays – Dungarvan and Donegal Bay – account for over 50 per cent of oyster production in the country. These bays are ideal for oyster culture, with excellent tidal exchange and perfect conditions for creating high-quality meat content and flavour. Indeed, every bay that cultivates oysters is unique and will offer distinct flavours, from the clean, fresh taste of a Carlingford to the sweet plumpness of a Bannow oyster. With over forty bays around Ireland producing oysters, there is sure to be one that suits every palate.

Let the journey begin.

Richard Donnelly
Aquaculture Business Development Manager
Bord Iascaigh Mhara
Irish sea fisheries development board

Opening or shucking oysters

Check that the oysters have firmly closed shells. They should feel heavy when lifted. Discard any that are cracked or damaged. Scrub the live oyster shells with a stiff brush under cold running water.

1 Holding the oyster firmly on a firm surface, insert the oyster knife into the gap at the hinge.

2 Slowly work the blade in and twist it slightly to prise the hinge apart.

3 Slide the blade along the top flat shell to sever the muscle. Discard the top flat shell.

4 Dislodge the oyster from the shell, being careful not to spill any of the juices. Check for bits of shell or grit.

5 Use the bottom curved shell for presentation and serving of a beautiful oyster swimming in juice.

Native and rock oysters

Native oyster / European flat shell *Ostrea edulis*

Rock / Pacific oyster *Crassostrea gigas*

I love oysters. It's like kissing the sea on the lips.

Leon-Paul Fargue (1876–1947)

Kilkieran Bay, Co. Galway

The Original

Recipes by **Máirín Uí Chomáin**

*Photography by **Walter Pfeiffer***

Oyster cuisine Máirín Uí Chomáin

In 2004 I had the great pleasure to write a book entitled *Irish Oyster Cuisine* which was published by A&A Farmar. It went on to win the World Gourmand Cookbook Award for Best Fish Book, and I took a memorable journey to Sweden to accept the award and – most importantly – to meet other food writers and authors. The book was well received at home too, and was named Foodbook of the Year 2005 by *Food & Wine* magazine. Over the years, it went out of print, and as I viewed with great joy the renaissance in interest in oysters, it saddened me that my book was no longer available.

Some years later, I was invited by the Connemara Mussel Festival committee to develop a book of mussel recipes. In creating that book, *Irish Mussel Cuisine*, I had the good fortune to meet up with Vincent Murphy, its designer, and Mary Ruddy, its recipe editor. They were establishing a publishing house in Connemara, and my book *Celebrating Irish Salmon* was to be their first publication. Working with them on this new book afforded me the great pleasure of collaborating again with Walter Pfeiffer, who had created the wonderful photography for *Irish Oyster Cuisine* which contributed in no small way to the success

of that book. Sadly, Walter died unexpectedly in April 2017 and so was unable to work on this book as had been planned. He is much missed.

In 2016, another title published by Artisan House, *Sea Gastronomy: Fish and Shellfish of the North Atlantic* by Michael O'Meara won the World Gourmand Cookbook Award for Best Fish Book – the same award I had won some 12 years earlier. We both live in Galway, Michael in the city where he is chef and patron with his wife Sinéad of the wonderful fish restaurant Oscar's Seafood Bistro. And we share the same publisher. It seems we were destined to work together, and the result is *Oyster Gastronomy*. Michael brings ideas and ingredients he encounters in his work as a full-time working chef. My recipes were developed from home using ingredients available in abundance to us from childhood.

Since my earliest days the sea has coaxed me. From the back steps of my childhood home in Connemara, I could literally dip my toes in the waters of Galway Bay. Exploring the seashore and its many forms of life through daily and seasonal change became a source of pleasure and constant wonder to me.

One of our clan, Seamus Mac An Iomaire, had published *Cladaigh Chonamara*, an excellent guide to the shores of Connemara. It was a revelation to me that features of our humble surroundings could be the basis for a book. Although I did not realise it then, this was an early inspiration to me to discover more about our maritime heritage and subsequently to write about the fish, shellfish and seaweeds which were part of the family diet. Later, as a young home economist, I had, as one of my first assignments, the task of training young Aran fishermen to cook well for themselves during their long stays at sea.

With marriage came a move to Dublin and, for a while, to the US. In America I saw how well various ethnic groups treasured their own native dishes, a clear hint that the island of Ireland could be more imaginative in using its seafood resources. Passing years, more changes of location and family commitments made for a jagged career path, but offered many fulfilling experiences in teaching, commercial food advisory services, catering and the media. Then fortune favoured me once more when I was able to return again and set up home within an oar's length of the Galway shoreline – the ideal setting to create a book celebrating the gifts of our coastal and marine resources.

Oysters, native and rock, are found in now wonderfully managed and operated oyster beds around our coasts and are worthy of celebration and of their well-deserved reputation for excellence. As outlined in Richard Donnelly's foreword, oysters have long been enjoyed in Ireland and continue to be enjoyed. They are rich in iodine, phosphorus and zinc, all of which add nutritional value to a diet.

We commonly think of consuming oysters by eating them raw in their half shells, washing them down with a few draughts of a good Irish beverage. In this way, they are indeed a treat. But can I entice you to be a little more venturesome? Oysters are very versatile in their culinary uses and can be enjoyed in a variety of settings – at breakfast, lunch, brunch, supper and as finger food at any time of the day. There are many possibilities for cooking and presenting oysters. The recipes are not difficult. I suggest you start with the soups: they are intended to get you hooked with their strong briny flavour. But however you choose to consume your oysters, know you are imbibing a highly nutritious and healthy food and a memorable gastronomic experience. To heighten the experience, try some of the beverage pairings suggested in Betty Murphy's notes, and as the French might say, *Voila, c'est la vie*, or *Sláinte*, as I might say.

Oysters au naturel

Serves 4

24 oysters
Crushed ice and/or seaweed
1 lemon, cut into wedges

Method
Scrub and rinse the oysters well.
Open them carefully with an oyster knife-try not to spill the juices.

Cover a large platter with crushed ice or seaweed (or both).
Carefully arrange the oysters and lemon wedges around the platter.

Serve with a Champagne or stout.

Oysters with smoked salmon

Serves 6-8

24 oysters in half shells
2 slices smoked salmon
2–3 tablespoons mayonnaise *(see p.107)*
1 teaspoon lemon juice
Garnishes
24 small strips of smoked salmon
1 tablespoon chives, chopped
Accompaniments
dulse brown bread *(see p.112)*
salted butter

Method
Blend the salmon, mayonnaise and lemon juice in a food processor until smooth.
Spoon the salmon mixture over the oysters.

Garnish with the salmon strips and chives and serve with buttered dulse bread.

Oyster soup

Served in demitasse cups, this frothy broth is a delectable beginning to an elegant meal.

Serves 4

12–18 oysters, shells removed, juices strained and reserved
225 ml milk
225 ml cream
25 g butter
dash of Tabasco
salt
black pepper, freshly ground
Garnishes
paprika
fingers of buttered toast

Method
Chop the oysters. Bring the milk, cream and butter to the boil in a saucepan, stirring continuously.
Lower the heat slightly, add the chopped oysters, juices, Tabasco, salt and pepper and heat through.

Ladle the soup into warm soup bowls, sprinkle with a little paprika and serve at once with the toast.

Note: You can aerate the soup before adding the oysters by using a hand whisk. This will make the soup more frothy.

Oyster bisque

Serves 4

12 oysters, chopped if large, juices reserved
3 tablespoons butter, melted
4 tablespoons white wine
25 g onion, chopped
25 g celery, chopped
25 g cornflour or plain flour
25 g button mushrooms, chopped
110 g prawns or shrimps, cooked and shelled
3 dashes of Tabasco
1–2 drops of Worcestershire sauce
425 ml milk
300 ml double cream
Garnish
6 additional oysters, shells removed

Method
Combine milk and oyster juice. Place all the ingredients except the oysters, the milk/oyster juice mixture and the cream in a food processor.

Add half the milk/oyster juice mixture and blend until smooth. Pour into a saucepan and cook with the rest of the milk/oyster juice for 6–8 minutes, whisking well. Mix in the cream and the chopped oysters and reheat very gently. Take care not to boil the bisque or the oyster meat will toughen.

Ladle into warm bowls and top with an oyster (you can leave the oysters raw or heat them for 1–2 minutes under the grill to plump them up).

Oysters florentine

Serves 6-8

24 oysters, shells removed and retained
90 ml mornay sauce *(see p.106)*
50 g butter
225 g spinach, washed and torn
salt
black pepper, freshly ground
Garnish
paprika
Accompaniment
sea vegetable muffins *(see p.113)*

Method
Make the mornay sauce and keep warm.
Melt the butter in a saucepan and sauté the spinach until it wilts. Season to taste.
Preheat the grill to high. Place the oyster shells on a baking tray. Cover each shell with a layer of buttered spinach.

Place an oyster on top and spoon some mornay sauce over each one.
Grill the oysters until the tops are glazed and golden (8–10 minutes).

Sprinkle with a little paprika and serve with sea vegetable muffins.

Note: crushed tinfoil on the baking tray will keep the oysters steady while cooking.

Oysters with boxty

A wonderful contrast of succulent oysters with golden potato boxty.
The humble potato is transformed into a sophisticated starter
or light lunch, worthy to be served with oysters and cream.

Serves 4

12–16 oysters, shells removed
Boxty
2 large potatoes, peeled
25 g plain flour
1 egg, beaten (optional)
pinch of salt
sunflower oil and butter for frying
Garnish
sour cream

Method
Coarsely grate the potatoes into a bowl, season with salt and add the flour and
egg, if using. Mix thoroughly. Heat the oil and butter in a heavy frying pan over
moderate heat. Fry the potatoes in spoonfuls, turning until golden on both sides.
Toss the oysters in the hot pan for about a minute to firm them.

Place the boxty on warm plates, add a dollop of sour cream and top with
the warmed oysters.

*Note: the egg makes the boxty lighter and adds to the food value, but boxty
without egg is more traditional.*

Oyster soufflé

Serves 4

12 oysters, shells removed, finely chopped
butter for greasing
50 g Parmesan
3 small eggs, separated
210 ml béchamel sauce *(see p.106)*
salt
black pepper, freshly ground

Method
Preheat the oven to 180 °C / 350 °F / gas mark 4. Grease four individual soufflé/ramekin dishes with butter and dust with a little of the cheese.

Whisk the egg yolks into the hot béchamel sauce off the heat. Add the remaining cheese and season with salt and pepper.

In a very clean bowl, whisk the egg whites with a pinch of salt until stiff.
Add a little of the egg white and the oysters to the cheese mixture and mix well. Very gently fold in the remaining egg whites. Divide the soufflé mixture amongst the dishes and bake for about 15 minutes until firm and brown on top.

Serve the soufflés straight from the oven with fingers of toast accompanied by a glass of chilled white wine.

Oysters oriental style

Serves 4

12–16 oysters in shells, scrubbed
1 small carrot, grated
1 thin slice of fresh ginger, finely grated
2 tablespoons light soy sauce
1 tablespoon sherry
½–1 teaspoon Tabasco
1–2 teaspoons sesame oil
2 scallions, cut into fine strips
Garnish
sprigs of parsley or coriander

Method
Blanch the carrot in boiling water for 1 minute, adding the ginger for the
last few seconds of blanching. Drain.

Mix the soy sauce, sherry, Tabasco and sesame oil together in a bowl.
Mix in the carrot, ginger and scallions.

Steam the oysters until the shells open slightly (3–4 minutes, depending on size).
Using an oyster knife, twist off the top shell.

Arrange the oysters on a platter and spoon the sauce over them.
Garnish with parsley or coriander and serve immediately.

Oysters with bacon

This is one of the best ever finger foods and another version of angels on horseback. It is better to par-cook de-rinded bacon rashers first before using them for wrapping the oysters, to make sure they are fully cooked.

Serves 4

12 oysters, shells removed
6 streaky bacon rashers, rinds removed,
cut in half and stretched
Garnishes
6 slices of toast, buttered and halved into triangles
sprigs of watercress or parsley

Method
Preheat the grill to high or the oven to 220 °C / 425 °F / gas mark 7.
Wrap the bacon around the oysters and slip on to skewers to secure.
Grill or bake the oysters for 5–6 minutes, turning occasionally to cook evenly.

Remove the oysters from the skewers and arrange on the triangles of toast.
Garnish with watercress or parsley and serve immediately.

Note: you can plump up the oysters by heating them in their own juices for a minute or two before wrapping the bacon around them.

Charming oysters I cry:
My masters, come buy,
So plump and so fresh,
So sweet is their flesh,
No Colchester oyster
Is sweeter and moister:
Your stomach they settle,
And rouse up your mettle:
They'll make you a dad
Of a lass or a lad;
And madam your wife
They'll please to the life;
Be she barren, be she old,
Be she slut, or be she scold,
Eat my oysters, and lie near her,
She'll be fruitful, never fear her.

Jonathan Swift (1667-1745)

Another Twist

Recipes and photography

by Michael O'Meara

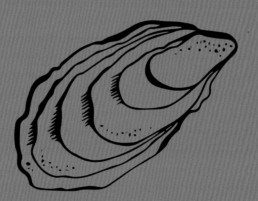

Oysters with panache Michael O'Meara

'Just eat the thing! How are you supposed to serve something if you have no idea how it tastes?' This is a common instruction in the kitchen to a new commis chef just out of cookery school. 'And don't stick the oyster knife through your hand' is the usual follow-up. A week or so later, the conversation is more like: 'Stop eating the bloody oysters – they're for the customers!'

As I write this, a new chef in the restaurant is counting every oyster he opens (1,850 so far), timing the speed of the shuck and just getting into one of the great culinary skills: opening oysters with panache. There's something special about oysters and always has been; they truly afford the culinarian the opportunity for showmanship.

The oyster is a bivalve mollusc that makes its home in marine and often brackish waters. Oysters are cultivated in tidal inlets and feed twice a day on the phytoplankton and algae in the surge of fresh seawater that washes over them with the incoming tide. They feed by filtering water through their gills by beating fine protuberances called cilia. Temperature is important for both spawning and feeding, with the optimum being slightly above 10°C. A single oyster can filter five litres of water per hour, so a pristine environment is of the utmost importance: any pollutants will concentrate in the body of the shellfish.

Environmental factors are more influential than species type on the taste of the oyster. Taste an oyster as you might a wine: it is subjective and personal, and takes time to develop. As with wine tasting, the terroir delivers a distinctive smell, taste and finish: is the oyster briny, vegetable or metallic, for example. The water salinity, nutrient mix, temperature and tidal conditions combine to determine how an oyster tastes. And like a fine wine, with practice it is possible to identify an oyster's origin by taste alone.

Oysters are always bought live. Traditionally they were eaten only during the months with the letter 'r' – September to April. This now applies only to the European flat shell or native oyster, as it spawns during the summer months so its quality then is not optimum. With modern methods of oyster farming, refrigeration and transport, it is possible to enjoy oysters at any time of year.

Proper storage is vital, as oysters are sensitive to temperature and light. The ideal temperature range for safe storage of oysters is 4–6°C. Resting the oyster cup-side up is critical and a legal requirement in the European Union when selling oysters. It allows them to retain their own reservoir of water, almost like a personal life support system. I have seen European flats with their shells secured closed with elastic bands – a good idea, in my opinion, since it's all about keeping the shellfish wet. Seaweed is easily the best medium on which to place oysters, and acts a little like its natural habitat. Of course, consuming any shellfish as soon as possible is recommended, but when stored correctly, oysters can last comfortably for a week.

To eat an oyster, I advise having your first one 'naked' – that is, without supplementing it – so you can ascertain the quality and taste, and I recommend that you chew a little, rather than slurp only, to bring up the full flavour. This will enable you choose the condiments and dressings, if any, that best suit its flavour.

Fresh and live oysters glisten in their shells and should feel quite heavy, as they should be full of water. If you are served a dry oyster in its half-shell, return it. It is obviously too long out of the water or was stored badly, and will have lost its succulence and flavour. Nowadays, oysters are most often eaten live and raw, dressed only with a squeeze of lemon juice or mignonette dressing. But they can be cooked and used in hot and cold dishes. Oysters can be steamed, poached, grilled, roasted or barbecued; they can be used in soups, casseroles, kebabs, even a sandwich. Oysters are versatile, and as you will see in this book, they lend themselves to all forms of cooking and to many flavours. I have no argument that the best way to enjoy an oyster is raw and with minimal intervention, but a bit of variety adds its own spice.

The most treasured oysters are the native oysters. Until relatively recently, they were the more commonly available, but now the larger meaty rock oyster has taken over.

Always buy really fresh oysters. Once harvested but not shucked, unopened oysters will last for up to a week if kept chilled and moist.

Oysters with pickled rock samphire and wild mustard flowers

Wild seashore ingredients are perfect with oysters. Rock samphire has a distinctive, fragrant flavour and is related to the more common marsh samphire in name only. When pickled, rock samphire makes a good substitute for capers.

Serves 2-3

12 oysters, freshly shucked, in half shells
100 g fresh rock samphire
40 ml white wine vinegar
1 teaspoon caster sugar
5 coriander seeds
½ teaspoon fennel seeds
fresh mustard flowers as garnish (optional)

Method
Bring a pot of salted water to a rolling boil, and plunge the rock samphire into the water for 30 seconds. Remove the samphire and immediately cool it down in very cold water. Dry the samphire and place into a non-reactive bowl.

Heat the white wine vinegar in a pot with the fennel seeds, coriander seeds and sugar, just enough to allow the sugar to dissolve. Allow to cool and infuse for 1 hour. When cooled, pour the vinegar on to the samphire and mix well. Allow to marinate overnight before use.

To serve, simply place a little of the pickled rock samphire on to each oyster, and garnish with the spicy mustard flowers.

Steamed oysters with fresh
laurel and sage

Oysters take on the most delicate of flavours when steamed, and this method allows plenty of room for experimentation. I have used fresh sweet laurel and sage in the water, but almost any combination of herbs will work.

Serves 2-3

12 oysters, freshly shucked, in half shells
1 small branch of a laurel tree with around 10 leaves
4 large sprigs of fresh sage
1 lemon, cut into wedges

Method
To a shallow pan with a tight-fitting lid, add water to a depth of 1.5 cm.
Add the laurel and sage and bring to a simmering boil.

Carefully place the oysters in their shells into the water, cup side up, being careful not to spill any juices or allow any water into the oysters.
Place the lid on the pan and allow the oysters to steam for 3–4 minutes.

Remove the lid and place the oysters on a suitable serving dish. A bed of hot seaweed works well, as it keeps the oysters from toppling over. Serve straight away with lemon wedges, or try an accompaniment from the sauce section.

Oysters with Arabic-style preserved lemons

Preserved lemons are a great larder condiment and work a treat as an accompaniment to many foods. The lemons must be preserved a number of weeks before use.

Serves 2-3

12 oysters, freshly shucked, in half shells
10 lemons, unwaxed *(if you can't find unwaxed, wash the lemons in hot water to remove as much wax as possible)*
100 g sea salt
a little extra lemon juice, freshly squeezed

Method
Cut a cross in the lemons from top to bottom, but don't let the knife cut completely through. Gently pull the lemons open and sprinkle generously with salt, inside and out.

Pack the lemons tightly into a preserve jar, pushing down to allow their juice to pour – but don't push them to a pulp. Top the jar up with lemon juice, then seal. The jar should be rotated every few days as the lemons preserve.
After 3 weeks, the lemons will be good to eat.

To serve with oysters, remove a preserved lemon from the jar and rinse under cold running water to remove excess salt. Chop into small pieces and spoon on to the oyster. Garnish with fresh herb, such as fennel.

Oyster soup with garlic onions and cream

Serves 3-4

12 oysters, shucked and juices reserved
1 medium onion, peeled and chopped
1 clove garlic, finely chopped
15 g butter
1 medium potato, peeled and cubed
200 ml fish stock *(see p.111)*
60 ml dry white wine
100 ml cream
½ tomato, peeled, deseeded and cut into strips

Method
In a thick-based pot gently fry the onions in the butter, but don't allow them to colour. Add the garlic and potatoes and cook gently until the potatoes begin to soften. Add the white wine and reduce by half. Add the fish stock, simmer and reduce by one-third. Add the cream and the juice from the oysters and simmer for a further 5 minutes.

Blend and strain the soup and then return to a clean pot. Bring to a slow simmer, and just before serving add the whole oysters and allow them to cook for about 1–2 minutes. Serve straight away garnished with the tomato, some fresh herbs and freshly baked brown bread.

Oysters with lemon gin marinated cucumber

This twist on the modern serving of gin with cucumber gives a delightful freshness, countered with a slightly bitter gin and finished with a little lemon zest.

Serves 2

6 oysters, freshly shucked
100 g fresh cucumber, neatly diced
30 ml good gin
½ teaspoon lemon zest, finely diced
1 tablespoon lemon juice

Method
Place the cucumber and lemon zest into a non-reactive bowl, then pour in the gin and lemon juice. Allow to infuse for 2 hours in the refrigerator.

To serve, simply spoon the mixture around the oysters in their shells – it really doesn't get any easier.

Oysters

Bloody Mary

This spicy oyster shot has become fashionable of late, and for good reason. Fresh tomato rather than pre-bought tomato juice gives a more flavoursome result.

Serves 3-4

12 oysters, freshly shucked, in half shells
2 ripe tomatoes
1 shot good-quality vodka
1 tablespoon Worcester sauce
1 tablespoon Tabasco sauce
1 ice cube
1 scallion, finely chopped
fresh celery leaves
salt
black pepper, freshly ground

Method
Blend the tomatoes, vodka and ice cube and pass through a fine strainer.
Season to taste with the Worcester and Tabasco sauces, and season
lightly with salt and freshly ground black pepper to make Bloody Mary.

Spoon a little of the Bloody Mary over the oysters, and garnish with
celery leaves and a few chopped scallions.

Kelly Oysters Kilcolgan, Co. Galway

Nestled in Killeenaran, a small inlet in Galway Bay, where the clean, clear waters provide ideal conditions for growing both native and rock oysters. The Atlantic seawater and the fresh water from the surrounding rivers combine to give the oysters a firm, meaty texture with a sharp mineral quality and dry palate finish.

Oysters with Yemeni green chilli zhoug

This hot and fragrant sauce from Yemen gives fresh oysters a whole new flavour profile, and is well worth trying.

Serves 2-3

12 oysters, freshly shucked, in half shells
4 teaspoons of zhoug sauce *(see p.100)*

Method
Simply spoon a little of the zhoug sauce over each oyster.

Oysters with citrus
and fennel

This fresh and fragrant combination adds great colour to an oyster display. The sweet orange counters the sharp lemon and lime, and combines well with the oyster's own brine and the fresh fennel.

Serves 2-3

12 oysters, freshly shucked, in half shells
2 sweet oranges, peeled and neatly segmented
½ lime, peeled and neatly segmented
½ lemon, peeled and neatly segmented
1 tablespoon good olive oil
fresh fennel sprigs

Method
Place the citrus fruit segments into a non-reactive bowl, and squeeze into the bowl any remaining juice after the segments were cut.
Add the olive oil and mix gently, ensuring the segments are not broken up.

Spoon two orange segments, half a lemon segment and one lime segment on to each oyster, and garnish with a sprig of fennel.

Seaweed steamed oysters

with Japanese-style dressing

This recipe uses a combination of seaweeds. I use sea lettuce and gutweed here, but other seaweeds, such as dried or fresh dillisk or pepper dillisk, work equally well. Bamboo steamers are ideal for steaming oysters and can be stacked on top of each other for efficient cooking.
You can serve the oysters directly from the steamer on to your table.

Serves 2-3

12 oysters, freshly shucked, in half shells
120 g fresh sea lettuce and gutweed
3 scallions, finely chopped
Japanese-style dressing *(see p.109)*

Method
Place the oysters, cup side up, into the steamer, being careful not to spill any of the juices. If you place the discarded top shells in first, they will help balance the cup side shells. Add a little sea lettuce to each oyster, and cover the steamer with its lid.

Bring a pot of water to boiling point. Once boiling, place the steamer on to the pot and cook for about 2 minutes at a high heat. To serve, sprinkle the oysters with the scallions and serve the Japanese-style dressing on the side as a dip.

Oyster pho soup

The fresh oysters and fragrant ingredients work perfectly together in this twist on the classic Vietnamese broth.

Serves 4-6

24 oysters, freshly shucked, removed from shells and with juices retained
200 g noodles, fresh udon or banh pho
100 g onion, peeled and thinly sliced
50 g fresh coriander leaves, chopped
2 red chillies, sliced
80 g bean sprouts
4 scallions, chopped
2 limes, cut into wedges
5 lime leaves
100 g spinach, washed and torn

Broth

3-inch piece of fresh ginger, cut lengthways
  into thick slices
1 cinnamon stick
½ tablespoon coriander seeds
½ tablespoon fennel seeds
3 star anise

4 cloves
2 black cardamon pods
1 tablespoon rock palm sugar
2 medium onions, skin on and quartered
1 litre fish stock *(see p.111)*
30 ml fish sauce

Method

Preheat the oven to 200 °C / 400 °F / Gas mark 6. Put a sheet of tinfoil on to an oven tray and roast the onions until well charred. You can also roast the onions on a non-stick pan with a little oil.

Add the cinnamon stick, cardamom, ginger, coriander, fennel seeds, star anise and cloves to a dry pan and roast carefully, being careful not to burn the spices. Add all the ingredients to the fish stock in a large stainless-steel pot. Bring the broth to a gentle simmer for about 1 hour, allowing the ingredients to infuse. Strain the broth into a clean pot.

Bring the pre-made stock to the boil, then add the noodles and chilli and cook for 1 minute. Add the bean sprouts and cook for a further 30 seconds. Add the remaining ingredients and simmer for 1 minute. Serve garnished with lime wedges.

Oyster

po'boy sandwich

A twist on the American classic, this sandwich shows how versatile oysters can be.

Serves 2

12 oysters, freshly shucked and removed from their shells
2 soft white hotdog rolls (use the best quality available)
50 g rice flour
50 g gram flour
¼ red onion, peeled and sliced
2 ripe vine tomatoes, sliced
100 g fresh salad greens, such as curly endive and rocket
2 tablespoons po'boy sauce *(see p.107)*

Method
Preheat a deep-fryer to 180 °C / 356 °F / Gas mark 4. Slice the rolls in half and toast until golden. Mix the gram and rice flour, and toss the oysters individually in the mixture. Then carefully deep-fry the oysters for about 1 minute or until they become firm and crisp.

Remove the oysters from the fryer and place on kitchen paper to soak up excess oil. Place the onions, salad greens and tomatoes on to the toasted rolls, then add a generous spoon of sauce. Top with the fried oysters and serve straight away.

DK Connemara Oysters Ballinakill Bay, Co. Galway

This farm can trace its ancestry back to 9 November 1893 when licence number 171 was granted to J McSheehy Esq for the entire Dawros peninsula. They farm rock oysters that are meaty and have a delightful sweet aftertaste which can be savoured on the open farm tour.

Roast oysters with

thyme-infused caramelised onions

This utterly delicious dish will tempt even the most reluctant oyster eaters.

Serves 2-3

12 oysters, freshly shucked, in half shells, juices discarded
1 large onion, peeled, halved and thinly sliced
20 ml sunflower oil
25 g salted butter
4 small sprigs of fresh thyme
salt to season

Method
Place the onions, thyme, butter and sunflower oil into a heavy pan. Cook slowly over a moderate heat until the onions are completely tenderised and take on a deep golden-brown colour. When cooked, season with a pinch of salt and place aside.

Preheat the oven to 200 °C / 400 °F / Gas mark 6 and place the oysters on a roasting tray. Alternatively, heat the barbecue until the coals are grey and hot. Put a generous spoonful of the onion mixture on to each oyster, then cook until the oysters and onions are piping hot. Serve straight away.

Adding a tablespoon of water to the onions early in the cooking will speed it up, especially if the pan becomes a little dry.

Roast oysters with

chorizo potatoes

This tasty dish has a deep, smoky flavour from the spiced sausage and is a great option for first-time oyster eaters. Allow six oysters per person.

Serves 2-3

12 rock oysters, freshly shucked, in half shells, juices discarded
200 g potatoes, pre-boiled and neatly diced to 5 mm
50 g good-quality chorizo sausage, cut to a similar size as the potatoes
2 shallots, peeled and diced
1 tablespoon olive oil

Method
Preheat the oven to 200 °C / 400 °F / Gas mark 6. Heat a non-stick pan with the olive oil, and add the shallots. Cook for 1 minute over a medium heat.

Add the potatoes to the pan and cook until they start to take on a light colour. Then add the chorizo and cook for a further 5 minutes, allowing the oils in the chorizo to coat the potatoes.

Spoon the potatoes into the oysters while still hot, then put the oysters on a roasting tray. Drizzle any excess juice from the potatoes over the oysters, and allow to mix with the oyster's juices.

Roast in the oven for about 5 minutes or until the oysters are just cooked, then remove from the oven and serve straight away.

Roasted oysters with zingy and

sweet quince jelly

Quince jelly is most often associated with cheese and cold meats, but add a squeeze of lemon juice and you get a nice sweet and sour sauce with zingy fruit notes. Fresh quince can be difficult to find, but quince jelly is readily available in most cheesemonger shops.

Serves 2-3

12 oysters, freshly shucked
1 lemon
6 teaspoons quince jelly *(see p.111)*

Method
Place ½ teaspoon of the quince jelly and a teaspoon of lemon juice on to each oyster.

Roast in a preheated oven at 200 °C / 400 °F / Gas mark 6 until the oysters are heated through, usually about 4 minutes.

Roasted oysters with

green gooseberries

Sour green gooseberries, lightly cooked and with a tiny pinch of sugar, make a great accompaniment to oysters and oily fish, especially mackerel.

Serves 2-3

12 oysters, freshly shucked, in half shells, juices discarded
80 g fresh green gooseberries, topped and tailed
2 tablespoons lemon juice, freshly squeezed
1 tablespoon caster sugar

Method
Place the gooseberries and sugar in a small pot and cook lightly until the gooseberries become tender – don't let them overcook and become a purée. Add the lemon juice at the last minute and put aside.

Preheat the oven to 200 °C / 400 °F / Gas mark 6 or, if available, light the wood oven. Spoon a few gooseberries and their juice on to the oysters and roast in the oven for about 4 minutes or until the oysters are just heated through. Serve straight away.

Oysters barbecue with puy lentil

and chilli paste

The lentils give a delicious earthy flavour to the oysters, and the hot kick of the chilli works a treat.

Serves 6-8

24 oysters, freshly shucked, removed from shells but with shells retained
150 g puy lentils, soaked in water overnight
1 medium carrot, peeled and diced
1 small onion, peeled and diced
3 sticks of celery, diced
20 g leek, cleaned and diced
30 ml olive oil
200 ml vegetable or chicken stock
2 cloves garlic, peeled and finely chopped
sprig of fresh thyme
basil leaves
salt
black pepper, freshly ground
chilli paste *(see p.104)*

Method
Into a heavy, suitably sized pot, add the olive oil, carrot, leek, onion and celery and fry over a moderate heat until the vegetables start to take on a light colour – about 10 minutes.
Add the lentils and mix through the vegetables. Add the garlic and thyme, then cook for a further 2 minutes. Add the stock and bring the lentils to a simmering boil. Allow to cook for 20 minutes, or until the lentils become soft and palatable but not overcooked.
Season with salt and black pepper and transfer to a suitable storage container. The lentils can be prepared in advance and will keep for 2–3 days in the refrigerator.

Preheat the oven to 200 °C / 400 °F / Gas mark 6, spoon a generous tablespoon of lentils into each oyster shell, and place the oyster on the lentils. Add a little of the chilli paste and fresh basil, and roast until the oysters are lightly cooked and hot. Serve straight away.

Grilled oysters with

chervil garlic butter

Chervil gives this classic butter a fragrant, aniseed-like finish that is a great match with freshly grilled oysters.

Serves 2-3

12 oysters, freshly shucked, in half shells, juices discarded
60 g salted butter, soft
½ lemon, juice
25 g fresh chervil
2 cloves garlic, peeled

Method
Put the butter, lemon juice, chervil and garlic into a food processor and blend to a smooth paste.

Put a small knob of butter on to each oyster, and place under a hot preheated grill or on the coals of a barbecue. Allow the butter to melt and boil while lightly cooking the oysters; this will take 2–5 minutes.

Serve straight away with freshly baked bread.

Carlingford Oyster Company Co. Louth

Located in Carlingford Lough, where there is an enormous exchange of water with each tide. This provides the nutrients on which the oysters thrive and have done so for millennia. Their oysters are sweet, with a slightly nutty flavour, followed by a suggestion of tannin and a lingering aftertaste.

Sauces and accompaniments

for oysters au naturel

The flavour of oysters is so wonderfully delicate and briny that they are best served well chilled, with just a squeeze of lemon juice. Not everyone may agree, however, and if you are serving oysters to guests, it is fun to vary the taste by offering a mixture of flavours with sauces and accompaniments.

The recipes here will be enough for at least 12 oysters, but for most of the sauces there will be a surplus. Many of the sauces will also work a treat with various other foods, so they won't go to waste.

Mignonette sauce

Mignonette sauce is a simple but classic condiment for oysters. Its basic ingredients are shallots, cracked pepper and vinegar. Here we offer three variations: traditional, sweet, and hot. The recipes are enough for 12 oysters.

Traditional mignonette

2 shallots, peeled and very finely chopped
½ teaspoon caster sugar
50 ml red wine vinegar
¼ teaspoon black peppercorn, freshly ground

Method
Combine the ingredients in a non-reactive bowl and allow to infuse for an hour before serving.

Sweet mignonette

2 shallots, peeled and very finely chopped
50 ml white wine vinegar
1 green apple, very finely diced
¼ teaspoon black peppercorn, freshly ground

Method As above.

Hot mignonette

2 shallots, peeled and very finely chopped
50 ml white wine vinegar
1 teaspoon sriracha sauce
¼ teaspoon black peppercorn, freshly ground

Method As above.

Simply spoon a little of the mignonette over each oyster, or serve as a dipping sauce on the side.

Vierge salsa

70 g ripe vine tomatoes, chopped
5 good-quality black olives, de-stoned and quartered
10 capers, halved
½ lemon, juice
50 g basil leaves
30 ml good-quality olive oil

Method
Place the tomatoes, olives and capers into a
small pot and gently warm over a low heat.

Don't allow to stew. When warmed, add the
lemon juice and olive oil. Tear the basil leaves
and stir in just before serving.

**You needn't tell me that
a man who doesn't love
oysters and asparagus
and good wines has got a
soul, or a stomach either.
He's simply got the instinct
for being unhappy.**

*Hector Hugh Munro,
better known by pen name 'Saki'
(1870–1916)*

Oriental mint and cucumber salsa

2 tablespoons cucumber, finely diced
½ red onion, finely diced
1 tablespoon fresh mint, chopped
2 tablespoons light soy sauce
2 tablespoons rice vinegar
2 tablespoons fresh lemon juice
1 teaspoon dried dillisk, rehydrated
and finely chopped

Method
Mix all the ingredients and allow to infuse
for 2 hours before use.

Salsa Mexicana

5 ripe plum tomatoes, finely diced
1 clove garlic, minced
1 medium-sized red onion, finely diced
2 limes, juice
2 tablespoons white wine vinegar
2 fresh jalapeño chilli peppers, deseeded and
finely chopped
50 g fresh coriander, chopped roughly
1 tablespoon olive oil

Method
Add all the salsa ingredients to a bowl, apart
from the coriander, and season with salt and
pepper. When you're satisfied with the
seasoning, add the coriander.

Cover with cling film and allow to infuse
outside the refrigerator for about an hour
before use.

Salsa de mani

**Salsa de mani is a savoury warm peanut
sauce from Asia.**

1 medium onion, finely diced
2 cloves garlic, minced
1 red pepper, deseeded and cut into strips
1 teaspoon ground cumin
1 tablespoon tomato purée
½ teaspoon dried oregano
420 g tinned tomatoes
3 tablespoons peanut butter
2 tablespoons olive oil
salt and black pepper, freshly ground

Method
Heat the oil in a pan and add the onion,
garlic and red pepper. Cook gently until
the onions and peppers soften. Add the
cumin, oregano, tomato purée and tomatoes
and bring the sauce to a simmering boil
for about 10 minutes. Stir in the peanut
butter, season to your liking and cook for
a further 7–10 minutes.

Zhoug

Zhoug is a very fragrant, hot and spicy herb and chilli pepper relish believed to have originated in Yemen.

Yemeni green chilli zhoug

8 green jalapeño chillies, deseeded
3 cloves garlic, peeled
25 g flat-leaf parsley, washed
25 g fresh coriander, washed
1 teaspoon cumin seeds
½ teaspoon ground coriander
100 ml olive oil
a little salt and black pepper, freshly ground

Method
Put the ingredients into a blender and purée to a smooth paste. Put into a bowl, cover, and refrigerate for a few hours to allow the flavours to infuse.

Bravas sauce

1 onion, finely chopped
2 garlic cloves, finely chopped
50 ml dry white wine
400 g canned tomatoes
2 teaspoons red wine vinegar
1 teaspoon crushed dried chillies
2 teaspoons smoked paprika
10 ml olive oil
salt and pepper, freshly ground

Method
Add olive oil to a medium-sized pot and sauté the onion for about 5 minutes until soft. Add the garlic, fry for 30 seconds, then add the vinegar, wine, tomatoes, dried chillies and smoked paprika. Simmer for 20 minutes over a low heat, then blend until smooth. Season with a little salt and pepper and place aside.

Thai vinaigrette

1 teaspoon lemongrass, finely chopped
1 teaspoon coriander leaf, chopped
1 tablespoon chives, finely sliced
½ teaspoon Thai bird's eye chilli, finely chopped
2 tablespoons Thai fish sauce (nam pla)
1 teaspoon light Thai-style soy sauce
75 ml sunflower oil
30 ml rice wine vinegar

Method
Whisk all the ingredients together and allow to infuse in the refrigerator for 3 hours before use.

Accompaniments for
cooked oysters

It's hard to beat freshly shucked oysters enjoyed au naturel. However, for oyster virgins, cooked oysters may be a gentler introduction.

Oysters can successfully be steamed, grilled, stewed or roasted and the book includes recipes for a wide variety of cooking methods. For some of these methods, the oysters need to be shucked first and shucking oysters can be time-consuming. If you're catering for a crowd, barbecuing oysters in their shells is a great option. The heat pops them open, and they can be served straight from the grill with an accompanying sauce.

Smoked paprika barbecue sauce

It's difficult to make a small amount of barbecue sauce, but the recipe on this page is very versatile and will work with any meat or fish. It makes 70 ml of sauce, which can be stored safely for two weeks in the refrigerator.

Stage 1

1 medium onion, peeled and diced
100 ml white wine vinegar
50 ml caster sugar
40 ml honey
1 teaspoon fennel seed
½ teaspoon black pepper, freshly crushed
½ teaspoon coriander seed
1 red chilli pepper
4 cloves garlic, peeled

Method
Combine the ingredients in a non-reactive bowl and allow to infuse for an hour before serving.

Stage 2

50 ml tomato purée
30 ml dark soy sauce
200 g tinned pineapple in syrup
3 tablespoons smoked paprika
salt to season

Method
Add the stage 2 ingredients to the sauce and simmer for 30 minutes. If it thickens too much, add a little water. Then blend the sauce and pass it through a fine strainer. Season lightly with salt, allow to cool and store in the refrigerator until needed.

Balsamic Teriyaki sauce

50 ml balsamic vinegar
100 ml chicken stock
25 g sugar
2 tablespoons soy sauce
2 tablespoons mirin
1 teaspoon arrowroot

Method
Put the balsamic in a non-reactive pot and reduce by two-thirds. Add the stock, sugar, soy sauce and mirin, and simmer until the sugar dissolves. Mix the arrowroot with a little water, then add to the sauce to thicken it. Serve as a dip with freshly steamed oysters.

Chilli vinegar dipping sauce

2 hot chilli peppers, finely sliced
100 ml white wine vinegar
2 teaspoons Thai fish sauce (nam pla)

Method
Combine the ingredients and allow to infuse in the refrigerator for 2 hours before use. This sauce is good with fresh raw oysters and steamed oysters.

Chilean pebre sauce

2 hot chilli peppers
(e.g., bird's eye, Habanero or Scotch bonnet)
100 ml olive oil
1 small onion, finely chopped
2 tablespoons coriander, chopped
3 tablespoons flat parsley, chopped
4 cloves garlic, peeled and chopped
2 teaspoons fresh oregano, chopped
5 tablespoons red wine vinegar
salt and black pepper, freshly ground

Method
Add all the ingredients to a blender, and blitz to a fine but textured purée. Place in a bowl, cover with cling film, and allow to infuse in the refrigerator for 24 hours before use. This sauce is good with raw, steamed, grilled or fried oysters.

Chilli paste

1 bell pepper, roasted and peeled
2 red chilli peppers, roasted
2 gloves of garlic, peeled
20 ml olive oil
salt to season

Method
Put all the ingredients into a blender, and blitz to a smooth paste.

Lime ponzu

1 lime, zest and juice
2 tablespoons rice wine vinegar
1 tablespoon light Japanese soy sauce
2 teaspoons mirin
1 teaspoon sugar
3 tablespoons sake
1 tablespoon dried kelp, dillisk or any kombu
1 tablespoon ginger, peeled and minced

Method
Put all the ingredients in a bowl, and whisk until
the sugar dissolves. Cover with cling film and allow
to infuse in the refrigerator for 24 hours. This sauce
is a good dip with cooked or raw oysters.

Tamarind sauce

170 g tamarind pulp
1 bird's eye chilli
1 teaspoon ginger, peeled and minced
50 g brown sugar
2 tablespoons honey
1 tablespoon soy sauce
1 tablespoon fresh garlic, minced

Method
Put the tamarind into a bowl, just cover with
boiling water, and soak for 3 hours. Push the pulp
through a sieve into a stainless-steel pot, and
add the remaining ingredients. Bring to a gentle
simmer for 3 minutes, then remove from the heat
and allow to cool. This sauce is particularly good
with barbecued, roasted or steamed oysters.

Nuoc Mam Cham Vietnamese dipping sauce

125 ml coconut water
2 tablespoons rice vinegar
2 tablespoons palm sugar
2 cloves garlic, crushed
4 bird's eye chillies, finely chopped
½ lime, juice
2 tablespoons Vietnamese fish sauce
(nuoc mam)

Method
Put the coconut water and sugar in a non-
reactive pot and bring to the boil. Remove
from the heat and allow to cool. Add the
remaining ingredients and allow the sauce
to infuse outside the refrigerator for 2
hours before use. This sauce is good with
any fried or steamed oyster.

Mornay
sauce

50 g butter
25 g plain flour
pinch of salt
300 ml milk
2 teaspoons fresh cream
75 g farmhouse cheese, grated

Method
Put all the ingredients in a saucepan, place over a medium heat and using a balloon whisk, keep whisking until the sauce is cooked and thickened. This works for me always and is a very fast method.

Note: if you want a very rich mornay sauce, whisk in 1 egg yolk with the cream. This is a good glazing sauce for grilled oysters.

Béchamel
sauce

300 ml pint milk
1 medium onion, peeled
1 bay leaf
5–6 white peppercorns
25g butter
25g plain flour
pinch of salt

Method
Pour the milk into a saucepan, add the onion, bay leaf and peppercorns and simmer over a very low heat for 5–10 minutes until the flavours infuse. Strain the milk into a jug or bowl discarding the peppercorns, onion and bay leaf.

Put the milk and the remaining ingredients into a saucepan, place over a medium heat and using a balloon whisk, keep whisking until the sauce is cooked and thickened.

Hollandaise
sauce

3 tablespoons white wine vinegar
6–8 peppercorns
1 blade mace
1 bay leaf
4 egg yolks
pinch of salt
110 g butter, melted
lemon juice

Method
Place the vinegar, peppercorns, mace and bay leaf in a saucepan and simmer over a low heat until reduced to one-third. Strain.

Put the egg yolks, reduced vinegar mixture and salt into a liquidiser.

While the motor is running, add the melted butter in a slow stream.

Finally, add lemon juice to taste. Pour into a warm jug and stand in a bowl of hot water to keep the sauce warm.

Mayonnaise

2 egg yolks
300 ml olive oil
1 teaspoon lemon juice
salt and white pepper

Method
Put the egg yolks and salt in a blender. Blend a little and with the motor still running, very slowly pour in the oil until you get the correct consistency.

As the mayonnaise thickens the oil can be added a little faster.

Add the lemon juice and season to taste.

Po'boy sauce

60 ml mayonnaise
30 ml tomato ketchup
½ teaspoon sweet paprika
1 tablespoon Worcester sauce
1 tablespoon Tabasco sauce
1 tablespoon brandy (optional)

Method
Whisk all the ingredients together and put aside.

Ginger salsa

1 small red onion, finely chopped
2 tablespoons fresh ginger, very finely chopped
1 tablespoon light soy sauce
3 tablespoons rice vinegar
½ teaspoon bonito flakes

Method
Mix all the ingredients and allow to infuse in the refrigerator for 2 hours before use. This sauce is good with fried or steamed oysters.

Kachumber salsa

3 ripe vine tomatoes, halved and thinly sliced
1 small onion, peeled, halved and thinly sliced
2 tablespoons fresh coriander, coarsely chopped
¼ teaspoon cumin seed, crushed
pinch cayenne or chilli powder
1 tablespoon white wine vinegar
salt to season

Method
Mix all the ingredients and allow to infuse in the refrigerator for about 1 hour before use. This sauce is good with raw or steamed oysters.

Sardinia almond and caper salsa

50 g almonds, blanched, peeled and lightly toasted
20 g capers, drained
¼ teaspoon dried chilli flakes
70 ml good-quality olive oil
1 clove garlic, minced
20 g mint leaf
1 lime, juice

Method
Put the almonds, capers and chilli flakes into a blender and blend to a rough paste.

Heat the oil in a pan over a low heat, add the garlic and mint, and sauté for 30 seconds to infuse the flavours. Remove from the heat and allow to cool.

Add the infused oil to the almond paste in the blender, and blend until an emulsion is formed. Finish with the lime juice and allow to cool completely before serving.
This sauce is good with fried, steamed or grilled oysters.

Salsa ranchero

This sauce is great with grilled and barbecued oysters.

2 tablespoons sunflower oil
1 small onion, peeled and finely diced
1 tablespoon garlic, finely minced
1 chilli pepper, finely chopped
7 ripe vine tomatoes, chopped roughly
1 teaspoon tomato paste
1 teaspoon sugar
1 teaspoon cumin, finely ground
1 teaspoon fresh oregano, finely chopped
1 tablespoon coriander, chopped

Method
Heat a heavy pan and add the oil and onion.
Cook for about 5 minutes until the onion
softens. Add the garlic and chilli and cook
for a further 5 minutes. Add the tomatoes,
tomato paste, cumin, sugar, oregano and
coriander and simmer for another 10 minutes.

Japanese - style dressing

3 tablespoons rice wine vinegar
1 tablespoon caster sugar
2 tablespoons Japanese mirin
2 tablespoons light Japanese soy sauce
2 tablespoons gin
1 tablespoon sushi ginger, chopped

Method
Place all the sauce ingredients in a small,
non-reactive pot and bring to a slow simmer,
allowing the sugar to dissolve. Allow to cool.
Use with steamed oysters.

Tarragon dressing

25 g fresh tarragon, chopped
2 scallions, finely chopped
1 tablespoon white wine vinegar
1 tablespoon lemon juice
2 tablespoons good-quality olive oil

Method
Mix all the ingredients and allow to infuse in the
refrigerator for 30 minutes before use. This is a
good sauce for raw or steamed oysters.

Tangy plum chutney

A tangy chutney is a larder essential and helps make a great meal at short notice. This recipe will make far more chutney than is required for the oysters, but it will keep for many months in preserve jars.

10 ripe plums, deseeded and cut into small chunks
1 tablespoon fennel seed
1 tablespoon sunflower oil
150 ml cider vinegar
100 g brown sugar
1 medium onion, peeled and finely diced
1 tablespoon coriander seeds, crushed
1 cinnamon stick
1 tablespoon ginger, peeled and finely chopped
300 ml water
1 orange, juice and zest

Method
Prepare the preserve jars by boiling gently for 10 minutes with the lids off and rubber seal removed. Remove from the water, replace the seal, then close the jars until required.

Add the sunflower oil and onions to a non-reactive pot, and cook until the onions soften. Add the plums and cook for a further 5 minutes. Add the vinegar, sugar and remaining ingredients, and allow the chutney to simmer for 1 hour. Stir often, being careful not to let the bottom burn. If the chutney becomes dry, add a little water.

When cooked, remove the cinnamon stick and pour the chutney into the prepared jars. Seal the jars and allow the chutney to infuse for at least 1 week before use. There is no need to refrigerate unopened jars, but keep refrigerated once opened.

Dillisk and lime-leaf butter

2 tablespoons fresh or rehydrated dillisk seaweed
1 lemon, juice and zest
3 frozen kaffir lime leaves, shredded
100 g butter

Method
Place all the sauce ingredients in a small, non-reactive pot and bring to a slow simmer, allowing the sugar to dissolve. Allow to cool. Use with steamed oysters.

Fish stock

50 g celery, chopped roughly
100 g carrot, chopped roughly
1 large onion, chopped roughly
200 g leek, chopped roughly
3 kg turbot bones, cut into manageable pieces
10 whole black peppercorns
a generous sprig of fresh thyme
50 g flat-leaf parsley

Method
Wash the turbot bones under cold running water.

Place all ingredients into a large non-reactive pot and just cover with cold water.

Over a gentle heat bring the stock to a boil and simmer for 30 minutes.

Strain the liquid through a fine sieve using a ladle; do not pour the stock, as this may result in a cloudy finish.

This stock can be frozen in small batches for later use.

Quince jelly

1.5 kg fresh quince, cleaned and chopped, stems removed
sugar

Method
Put the quince into a large pot and just cover with water. Bring to the boil and simmer for about 1 hour until the fruit is cooked.

Mash the fruit with a potato masher and strain through a fine strainer. After initial straining to remove the heavy pulp, place the juice into a jelly bag and collect the juice overnight.

Measure the juice into a pot using a cup, and for each cup of juice stir in a cup of sugar. Bring the sugary juice to a gentle simmer, and boil until the syrup begins to gel.

To test the jelly, pour a little on to a cold plate and see if it sets.

When ready, pour into prepared preserve jars.

White kombu
crisps bread

225 g white self-raising flour
2 tablespoons kombu crisps or
  a mixture of sea vegetables, chopped
1 medium egg, beaten
2 tablespoons sunflower oil
150 ml milk (approx.)

Method
Preheat the oven to 190 °C / 375 °F / gas mark 5.
If using a fan oven, reduce the temperature by
10–15 degrees.

Grease a 23 x 11 cm loaf tin.
Mix the flour and sea vegetables together
in a bowl. In a separate bowl mix the beaten egg
and sunflower oil with the milk.

Make a well in the centre of the flour, pour in
the milk mixture and mix from the centre out
with a wooden spoon until all the ingredients
are combined.

Pour the mixture into the loaf tin and bake in
the centre of the oven for about 30 minutes.

Pierce the centre with a skewer.
If it comes out clean, the bread is cooked.
Cool on a wire rack.

*Note: if you need a larger loaf, double the
quantities and the size of the tin and bake
for 45 minutes.*

Dulse
brown bread

**Dulse (*Palmaria palmata*) known as
dilisc or *creathnach* is a sea vegetable.**
The earliest record of use of delicious dulse is by
St. Columba's monks approximately 1,400 years ago.

450 g ready-made Irish brown bread mix
25 g wheat germ
25 g oat bran
2 tablespoons dulse, finely chopped or ground
1 tablespoon pinhead oatmeal
450 ml fresh or sour milk
3 tablespoons sunflower oil

Method
Preheat the oven to 200 °C / 400 °F / gas mark 6.
Grease a 23 x 11 cm loaf tin.

Mix all the dry ingredients together in a bowl.
Mix the milk and oil together in a jug.

Make a well in the centre of the flour
mixture, pour in the liquid and mix from the
centre out with a wooden spoon until all the
ingredients are combined and the consistency
is quite wet.

Pour the mixture into the loaf tin and bake in the
centre of the oven for 40–50 minutes until the
loaf sounds hollow when tapped.
Cool on a wire rack.

Cheese
bread

450 g/1 lb self-raising flour
110 g Cheddar cheese, grated
2 medium eggs, beaten
4 tablespoons sunflower oil
1 teaspoon mustard (optional)
300 ml milk (approx.)

Method
Preheat the oven to 200 °C / 400 °F / gas mark 6.
Grease a 23 x 11 cm loaf tin.

Mix the flour and cheese together in a bowl.

Mix the beaten eggs, oil and mustard
together and pour the mixture into the
centre of the flour with enough milk to
make a very soft dough (too soft to handle).

Pour the mixture into the loaf tin and bake in the
centre of the oven for about 50 minutes.

Pierce the centre with a skewer and, if
it comes out clean, the bread is done.
Cool on a wire rack.

Sea vegetable
muffins

225 g white self-raising flour
2 tablespoons sea vegetables,
  finely chopped (kombu/dulse)
1 medium egg, beaten
3 tablespoons sunflower oil
150 ml milk

Method
Preheat the oven to 190 °C / 375 °F / gas mark 5.
Grease six muffin tins.

Mix the flour and sea vegetables together
in a bowl.

Mix the beaten egg with the oil and a few
tablespoons of the milk. Make a well in the
centre of the flour, pour in the egg mixture and
mix from the centre out with a wooden spoon.

Add enough of the remaining milk to make a
very soft dough. Spoon the mixture into greased
muffin tins and bake in the centre of the oven for
15–20 minutes.
Remove from the tin and cool on a wire rack.

*Note: cheese muffins can be made by replacing the sea
vegetables with 2 oz of grated Cheddar cheese.*

Anthony Coyne Oysters Outer Ballinakill Bay, Co. Galway

Anthony Coyne's oyster farm is located in Outer Ballinakill Bay under Letter Hill, with the backdrop of the quartzite-peaked Twelve Bens. Husband-and-wife team Anthony and Tricia farm rock oysters that are briny with a bright mineral tanginess.

Wild Atlantic Oyster Lissadell, Co. Sligo

Wild Atlantic Oyster is a collaborative brand involving three oyster farms in beautiful Sligo Bay, one at Coney Island, one at Lower Rosses and the third at Lissadell, an area made famous by W.B. Yeats and home of the Gore-Booth family. Indeed, the oyster fishery dates back to the 1860s when the Gore-Booth family established oyster beds, growing native oysters. Today the rock oysters farmed here combine a firm texture with a full, earthy flavour enhanced by the mineral-rich waters flowing from Ben Bulben.

The images feature the farm of Charles Kelly.

The Classics

Let's start with the queen of drinks to complement oysters: Brut champagne. A blanc de blancs made from the white chardonnay grape, it has the high acidity and citrus notes best suited to the briny oyster. Serve both lightly chilled, and the result is a royal feast – exquisite.

The main consideration is to taste both the oyster and the drink. An oyster is complex, with its salty juices and sweet, meaty flesh. So it's best to keep the beverage simple and pure, which does not at all mean tasteless and insipid. Think Chablis, a steely chardonnay from the cool north of Burgundy, or head farther north to the inner Loire, home to Sancerre and Pouilly-Fumé. These sauvignon blancs are dry, and again have high acidity and citrus flavours. No need for lemon wedges here, or your oyster will be drowned in lemon.

Head to the coast of the Loire and you will be in the Muscadet-Sèvre et Maine wine region. Aged on the 'lees', the post-fermented, dead yeast cells, Muscadet has a bready flavour and is so saline it almost tastes of the sea. Here, oyster stalls and Muscadet swigging are part of everyday life. Over-production and low-quality Muscadet are uninspiring, but experiment and pay a few euro more, as good producers are making a comeback.

If you're wondering why bone-dry, high-acidity, citrus wines work, try a low-acidity, off-dry, peachy wine such as

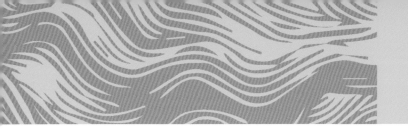

Pinot Grigio. It is always a matter of personal taste, but the oyster will most likely taste flabby and dull.

If champagne is the queen, stout is the king. Black Guinness, Murphy's and other burgeoning black stout varieties can't be beaten for palatable pleasure. The sweet-salt oyster flesh, coupled with the bitter, creamy texture of a 'pint of the black stuff', is an ever-astonishing gourmand experience and a visual delight. They complete each other.

Wines

For raw oysters, look out for a young vintage, again dry with high acidity and citrus fruit flavours so as not to overpower your oysters. The cool climate sparklings of Tasmania and the coasts of Australia and South Africa are a really good alternative to Champagne. A decent Spanish Brut Cava also works well. A Chilean chardonnay from the coastal region of Leyda is a suitable, inexpensive option for a large party, whereas your Premier Cru Chablis is gorgeous for a special date. Look out for the following wines if you want to experiment: Picpoul de Pinet, Verdejo, Albariño and Bordeaux or South African sauvignon-sémillon blends.

And on to some of my personal favourites. Try a dry tokaji, made from the furmint grape in Hungary. With its combination of fruit and minerality, this will marry well with both raw and cooked oysters. Riesling, young and pure from the Mosel, provided it is dry, is ideal for most of the dishes in this book. The Alsace varieties or those from Australia's Eden Valley are also superb. Next on my list is a Grüner Veltliner from Austria. Herbaceous with a slight tingle, it's my choice if there is ginger or spice in the recipe.

Last but not least, and it should come with a danger warning, is a fino or dry sherry, such as Manzanilla, from the coast near Jerez. 'Flor', a natural yeast in the sea air, is used in its production, and the result is a heavenly, dry, biscuity, nutty sherry. Luckily it's only 15 per cent alcohol by volume, low for a sherry, so pour a generous glass and enjoy. Make sure you buy a fresh young vintage, and once it's opened, drink up because it doesn't keep! It is divine with anything savoury, so it's extra good with the bacon-and-cheese-based oyster dishes.

Try These

Beers

An abundance of craft beers are waiting for your oysters. Once again, the oyster must take precedence. So choose beers that are light with apple and citrus tastes as opposed to the heavy, sweet and fruity varieties. A Pilsner Lager with oysters on the barbecue is sure to bring a summer feel, even in Ireland. The Porterhouse Oyster Stout is brewed with fresh oysters and is a smooth and velvety cushion for an oyster.

Gin and Vodka

If gin is your thing, go for the juniper- and citrus-dominant varieties such as the London Dry Gins.

Too many flowery botanicals could cloud your palate, and your oyster. I suggest less tonic, more ice and a frozen half of a lime, with a little fresh lime juice to taste.

Not being a vodka drinker, I was pleasantly surprised, during a recent visit to Dingle Distillery, by the purity of the vodka distilled from the spring water underneath the brewing house, which led to the Oyster-Shooter recipe. Freeze a good-quality vodka – it won't solidify. Pour a shot, add a couple of drops of Tabasco and down it with your chilled raw oyster. Alternatively, pop the shelled oyster into the glass and it will die happy.

Red Wine

A good quality Beaujolais Villages, such as a Morgon or Fleurie, is low in tannins and has a place to accompany the meat and cheese based oyster dishes. A Pinot Noir from Burgundy or New Zealand, or a Pinotage blend from South Africa are also low tannin wines. High tannins in heavy reds have a metallic effect on the palate a bit like having a cup of strong tea with an oyster. The delicacy may be lost.

When it comes to beverages, the world really is your oyster.

Before I was born my mother
was in great agony of spirit and
in a tragic situation. She could
take no food except iced oysters
and champagne. If people ask
me when I began to dance,
I reply, 'In my mother's womb,
probably as a result of the
oysters and champagne -
the food of Aphrodite'.

Isadora Duncan (1878 – 1927)

Contributors

Máirín Uí Chomáin Author

Connemara native Máirín Uí Chomáin is a former chair of the Irish Food Writers' Guild and an active member of the Slow Food movement. She holds an honorary MA from NUI Galway in recognition of her commitment to home economics. Máirín is the author of *Celebrating Irish Salmon* (Artisan House, 2013), *Irish Mussel Cuisine* (2011)and *Irish Oyster Cuisine* (A&A Farmar, 2004), which won the Gourmand World Cookbook Award for Best Fish Book 2004 and *Food & Wine* magazine Food Book of the Year 2005. Broadcaster Monty Halls, in the book accompanying the BBC series *Monty Halls' Great Irish Escape*, described Máirín as 'the high priestess of all matters pertaining to shellfish…A larger than life figure with the warmest of smiles and gentlest of accents.'

Michael O'Meara Author and photographer

Michael O'Meara is chef and patron of the multi-award-winning restaurant Oscar's Seafood Bistro, which he runs with his wife Sinéad in Galway city. He is an international award-winning photographer and Getty Images contributor. Michael holds a first-class-honours Master's degree in culinary innovation and was awarded the Dublin Institute of Technology Gold Medal for Academic Excellence. He is the author of *Sea Gastronomy: Fish and Shellfish of the North Atlantic* (Artisan House, 2015), which won the Gourmand World Cookbook Award for Best Fish Book 2016 and was nominated for Best Food Book of the Year 2015 in McKennas' Guide.

Walter Pfeiffer Photographer

Walter Pfeiffer was one of Ireland's foremost photographers. Originally from Eiffel in Germany, Walter lived in Ireland from 1964 until his unexpected death on 21 April 2017. Walter established himself in Dublin as a leading fashion and food photographer, working for major designers, food producers and marketers, including Bord Bia. His most recent work was to create the imaging behind Dunnes Stores' *Simply Better* brand. Walter created three highly regarded books of landscape photography: *Wicklow: A Personal View* (2000); *Connemara & Beyond* (2005); and *Connemara & Aran* (published posthumously by Artisan House, 2017). His photographs have appeared in numerous books and publications, including *Irish Oyster Cuisine* (A&A Farmar, 2004) and *Celebrating Irish Salmon* (Artisan House, 2013), both by Máirín Uí Chomáin; *New Irish Cooking* by Conrad Gallagher (A&A Farmar, 1997); *In the Houses of Ireland* (Thames & Hudson / Stuart Tabori & Chang / Abrams, 1988); *In an Irish Garden / L' Irlande: Un Art de Vivre* (Flammarion, 1986); and *Irish Cottages* (Weidenfeld & Nicolson, 1990).

Richard Donnelly Foreword

Richard Donnelly, Aquaculture Business Planning Manager with Bord Iascaigh Mhara (Irish Sea Fisheries Board), is responsible for business development with aquaculture enterprises, including oysters. Having extensive experience in the seafood sector, he is particularly passionate about the bivalve celebrated in this book and has worked with oyster producers in Ireland, USA and Asia. Oyster producers now provide the highest number of jobs in Irish aquaculture and are an industry vital to coastal communities.

Betty Murphy Beverage notes

Betty Murphy has a lifelong interest in wine and food which began when she was a language student in France. She hosts wine tastings and food pairings for small groups, and recently completed Level 3 of the international Wine and Spirit Educational Trust exams. Betty travels to wine-growing areas to deepen her understanding of the intricacies involved in the production of wine and associated spirits. Her plans involve completing her WSET studies, travelling more, and writing on her beloved topics of food and wine.

Books of *taste*
Created with *passion*
In the heart of *Connemara*

Award-winning Artisan House is based in Letterfrack, Connemara, Co Galway, Ireland. Established in 2013 Artisan House create beautifully illustrated high-quality books and bespoke publications on a richly diverse range of subjects including food and lifestyle, photography and the visual arts, music and poetry.

Creative *Vincent Murphy*   Editorial *Mary Ruddy*

Publications include:

Oyster Gastronomy
From two World Gourmand Award winning food writers
Máirín Uí Chomáin & Michael O'Meara (2017)

Tapestry of Light
Ireland's bogs and wetlands as never seen before
by photographer Tina Claffey (2017)

Connemara & Aran
by photographer Walter Pfeiffer (2017)

Letterfrack Poetry Trail
joint publication with CEECC (2017)

fermata
Writings inspired by Music
Editors: Eva Bourke and Vincent Woods (2016)

An Art Lover's Guide to the French Riviera
by Patrick J Murphy (2016)

The Mountain Ash
broadside by Joan McBreen & Margaret Irwin (2015)

Sea Gastronomy
Fish & Shellfish of the North Atlantic
by Michael O'Meara (2015)
(winner of Best Seafood Cookbook in the World Gourmand
Cookbook Awards 2016 and McKennas Guides Cookbook of the Year 2015)

Connemara
by Dorothy Cross (2014)

Joe Boske The Works
by Joe Boske (2014)

Celebrating Irish Salmon
by Máirín Uí Chómain (2013)

Artisan House Publishing Ltd.,
5 Ellis Workshops, Letterfrack, Connemara, Co Galway, Ireland.
email: artisanhouseeditions@gmail.com
www.artisanhouse.ie
Artisan House is a member of Publishing Ireland, *Foilsiú Éireann.*

Publisher's Acknowledgements

Artisan House gratefully acknowedges the support of Bord Iascaigh Mhara and of the West Fisheries Local Action Group for their support with this book. We offer a particular word of thanks to Séamus Breathnach and Caroline Curraoin for their assistance.

Oyster Gastronomy was originally conceived by Máirín Uí Chomáin. As she outlines in her introduction, it derived from her experience with the success of her previous publication, *Irish Oyster Cuisine* (A & A Farmar, 2004), now out of print. We are indebted to Máirín for coming to Artisan House with this concept, and it was our pleasure to have the opportunity to work with her again. Máirín's book *Celebrating Irish Salmon* was Artisan House's first publication in 2013 and holds a special place in our hearts.

We acknowledge with gratitude the cooperation of Anthony and Anna Farmar in providing us with text and images from *Irish Oyster Cuisine* and permission to use them.

The choice of a co-author for *Oyster Gastronomy* was an easy task. Michael O'Meara, like Máirín, was previously published by Artisan House, and again like Máirín, an award winner for his book *Sea Gastronomy: Fish & Shellfish of the North Atlantic*, which won the Gourmand World Cookbook Award for Best Fish Book 2016. Michael is a wonderful chef, an accomplished photographer and a proficient author. He is a delight to work with, and we wish to thank Michael and his wife, Sinéad, for their professionalism and cordiality.

This book is dedicated to Walter Pfeiffer, our dear friend and a professional photographer, who died unexpectedly on 21 April 2017. Walter worked with Artisan House on previous publications, most recently his superb book of landscape photography *Connemara & Aran* (2017), which sadly he did not see published. He worked on Máirín's previous oyster book, and we are so pleased to have his images, as he was a most ardent lover of oysters. Whenever Walter visited Connemara for a couple of days, we had to stock up on a minimum of five dozen oysters. We greatly regret that he is not with us to celebrate in a fitting way the publication of this book.

Richard Donnelly was not only an ideal foreword contributor but he also acted *ex officio* as our consultant, and we gratefully acknowledge his expertise and support.

Comparisons with wine occur frequently in the literature on oysters. We are fortunate to have found in Betty Murphy a knowledgeable enthusiast of both. Betty's beverage notes provide classic pairings as well as innovative suggestions: as she says, 'try it'.

We thank the oyster farms who allowed us to photograph their produce and their enterprise. The selection of farms gives an idea of the range of farm sizes in the Irish oyster sector – from a two-person operation to one employing almost twenty workers. But they all share a common feature: they are in stunningly beautiful coastal locations.

We are again indebted to Stan Carey for copy-editing and to Kate Murphy for indexing and proofreading. Thank you both for your meticulous work and for meeting challenging timeframes.

It is in the nature of publishing that those who are kind enough to provide a book endorsement get limited time to review that book. The endorsements of *Oyster Gastronomy* were supplied to us by highly respected people who live busy lives and have demanding schedules. We are most grateful to them for agreeing to take that time, and we are honoured to have such generous and positive responses from food writer, chef and patron, Richard Corrigan, Cliodhna Prendergast, *The Sunday Times* food writer, and from blogger extraordinaire and oyster sommelier, Julie Qiu. Thank you.

Co-funded by the Irish Government and the European Union
European Maritime & Fisheries Fund Operational Programme 2014-2020